Riddles

The best riddle book for clever kids

Table of Contents

Introduction

Thank you for choosing this book full of riddles for clever kids! In the following chapters you'll have fun trying to solve riddles on a range of topics, from Christmas riddles to number riddles. These riddles are sure to test even the cleverest kids, so think hard, good luck, and have fun!

Chapter 1: Animals and Vegetables Galore

Riddle: Why is the octopus laughing?
Answer: Because of ten tickles (tentacles)

Riddle: Why does a lion eat raw meat?
Answer: Because he can't be bothered to cook

Riddle: When a turtle marries a bird, what kind of baby will they have?
Answer: A turtle dove

Riddle: Where does a penguin keep his money?
Answer: Snow bank

Riddle: What does a lazy dog do to entertain himself?
Answer: He chases a parked car.

Riddle: My cow is on a holiday. Where is he?
Answer: He is in Moo York.

Riddle: Why does Mickey Mouse want to be an astronaut?
Answer: Because he wants to visit Pluto

Riddle: Why does a bee hum?
Answer: Because he does not know the lyrics

Riddle: A bird, squirrel, and monkey hungrily race up a coconut tree. Which of the three will make it to the banana first?

Answer: No one. There is no banana on the coconut tree.

Riddle: What is the monkeys' favorite month for playing baseball?
Answer: Ape-ril

Riddle: What is a rabbit's favorite mode of transportation?
Answer: Hare plane

Riddle: Why do bumble bees put honey underneath their pillows?
Answer: Because they want to have sweet dreams

Riddle: I always sleep with my shoes on. What am I?
Answer: A horse

Riddle: I am as big as a hippopotamus but weigh nothing at all. What am I?
Answer: The shadow of a hippopotamus
Riddle: What fur do you get from a lion?
Answer: As fur away as you can!

Riddle: Why do dragons prefer to sleep during the day?
Answer: Because they like hunting knights

Riddle: I honk but I don't have a horn. What am I?
Answer: A goose

Riddle: I have a horn but I don't honk. What am I?
Answer: A rhinoceros

Riddle: What is the biggest use for cowhide the world over?
Answer: To cover cows

Riddle: A horse with a 26-foot chain on his neck easily walked to an apple 30 feet away and ate it. How do you explain this?
Answer: The chain on the horse's neck was not tied to anything.

Riddle: When it is winter, what name will you give a bird?
Answer: Brrrrd

Riddle: How would you describe a grumpy cow?
Answer: It is a MOOdy cow.

Riddle: You will not want to play cards with this animal. What is it?
Answer: A cheetah

Riddle: What is a bear's favorite color for socks?
Answer: Nothing. A bear does not wear socks. He goes bare (bear) foot.

Riddle: A dog has fleas. What does a sheep have?
Answer: Fleece

Riddle: What does a frog do to stay happy?
Answer: He eats everything that "bugs' him.

Riddle: What do you call the eggs that wicked chickens lay?
Answer: Deviled eggs

Riddle: What makes you so sure that you should eat carrots for good eyesight?
Answer: Because you don't see any rabbit around who needs eyeglasses

Riddle: If a dog wants to stop watching a YouTube video, what does he do?
Answer: He presses the "paws" button.

Riddle: What is the T. Rex's favorite number?
Answer: The number "ate"

Riddle: When you find an elephant sitting on your fence, what time is it?
Answer: It is time to repair the fence or build a new one.

Riddle: When a bee goes near a flower, what does he say?
Answer: "Hello, honey!"

Riddle: What animal is able to jump higher than any building?
Answer: All animals can do this. A building isn't able to jump.

Riddle: You find yourself inside a cage with 3 monkeys. The 1st monkey is peeling a banana to eat. The 2nd monkey is playing with a stuffed toy. The 3rd monkey is working on the lock. Which of the primates inside the cage is the most intelligent one?
Answer: You

Riddle: What sounds like parrot and is orange in color?
Answer: A carrot!

Riddle: If a rabbit has fleas all over his body, what would you call him?
Answer: Bugs Bunny!

Riddle: What bird can tow a heavy load?
Answer: A crane

Riddle: What does a tiger always wear to bed?
Answer: His "paw"jamas

Riddle: What bird do you hear when you are eating?
Answer: A swallow

Riddle: Why didn't the other animals like to play baseball with the chickens?
Answer: Because the chickens always hit fowl balls

Riddle: Why do geese fly south for the winter?
Answer: Because it takes too long to walk there

Riddle: Which animal did the coach choose to hit the baseball?
Answer: A Bat

Riddle: What animal would you trust to always give you the right time?
Answer: A watch dog

Riddle: What animal has to use a nutcracker?
Answer: A toothless squirrel

Riddle: What bird would you use to help you write a letter?
Answer: A PENguin

Riddle: A dog accidentally sat on a sandpaper. What did he say?
Answer: Ruff!

Riddle: What do you call a cow that can't stop twitching?
Answer: Beef jerky

Riddle: How would you describe a left-handed dog?
Answer: A south paw

Riddle: What made the rabbit rich?
Answer: He found 24 carrots (karats).

Riddle: What do you call a cat with no legs to get him to come to you?
Answer: No matter what you call him, he won't be able to come to you.

Riddle: Billy has a fish with no eye. What kind of fish does Billy have?

Answer: FSH

Riddle: Peter owns an amazing dog detective. What name did Peter give his dog?
Answer: Sherlock Bones

Riddle: How do you describe a rabbit that jokes around a lot?
Answer: A funny bunny

Riddle: How do you describe a rabbit that has a really bad case of sniffles?
Answer: A runny bunny

Riddle: What do you call an alligator who steals big-time?
Answer: A crookodile

Riddle: What do you call a furious polar bear?
Answer: Don't call him anything. Just run!

Riddle: How do you describe two birds that are madly in love with each other?
Answer: Tweet hearts

Riddle: What happens when a bunny and bee get together?
Answer: You get a honey bunny.
Riddle: What do you get when a hedgehog gets together with a giraffe?
Answer: A toothbrush that is 6-foot tall

Riddle: What do you get when a snake gets together with a kangaroo?
Answer: A jump rope!

Riddle: What happens when you fill a rabbit hole with boiling water?

Answer: You get hot cross bunnies.

Riddle: What happens when a bear gets together with a skunk?
Answer: You get Winnie the Phew.

Riddle: What does an elephant need to date a fish?
Answer: Swimming trunks

Riddle: What happens when a rabbit gets together with a frog?
Answer: You get a bunny ribbit...ribbit...ribbit.

Riddle: What happens when a ghost gets together with a cat?
Answer: You get a scaredy cat!

Riddle: What do cats like to have for breakfast?
Answer: Mice krispies

Riddle: What game do frogs enjoy most?
Answer: Leapfrog

Riddle: What do puppies like to drink most?
Answer: Pupsi-cola

Riddle: What do you call a crocodile that is sick?
Answer: An ail-ligator

Riddle: What wins over a talking dog?
Answer: A spelling bee

Riddle: What do snakes like to study most in school?
Answer: Hiss-story

Riddle: When the rooster crowed, everybody in the world heard him. How do you explain this?

Answer: The rooster was in Noah's Ark.

Riddle: I have a beautiful terrier. Which side of my terrier has the most fur?
Answer: The outside

Riddle: What lies a hundred feet up but stays on the ground?
Answer: A dead centipede

Riddle: Why do the French enjoying eating snails?
Answer: Because they hate fast food

Riddle: What does the octopus hate to do?
Answer: Wash up before a meal

Riddle: Where do sheep go in summer?
Answer: The Baaaahamas

Riddle: Where does Mr. Mouse park his boat?
Answer: In the Hickory Hickory Dock

Riddle: From whom do dogs get their Christmas presents?
Answer: From Santa Paws

Riddle: Why does an elephant that works stays poor?
Answer: Because he works for peanuts

Riddle: Why is an elephant wrinkled?
Answer: Because he can't fit on an ironing board

Riddle: Why does an elephant have a trunk?
Answer: Because a bag is too small for him

Riddle: What happens when two silkworms run a race?
Answer: They have a tie.

Riddle: What do you get when you send your sheep off for karate lessons?
Answer: You get lamb chops.

Riddle: What game do frogs play when they get together?
Answer: Leapfrog

Riddle: Which one does not belong with the others: pelican, vulture, eagle, heron, hawk, or ostrich?
Answer: Ostrich, because he's the only which can't fly

Riddle: What does a nut say every time he sneezes?
Answer: Cashew

Riddle: Where do all the nuts go to borrow money from?
Answer: To the Cash-ew

Riddle: Which of the vegetables is considered the king of rock-and-roll?
Answer: Elvis Parsley

Riddle: What did the doctor tell the sick lemon to take?
Answer: Lemon-aid

Riddle: What fruit can never live by his lonesome?
Answer: A pear

Riddle: What fruit has a lot of fans?
Answer: Star apple

Riddle: What fruit is crazier and wackier than the other fruits?

Answer: The coco-nut

Riddle: What fruit is sweet and romantic?
Answer: The honeydew

Riddle: What vegetable stays miserable and takes a sour attitude to life?
Answer: The bitter gourd or bitter melon

Riddle: What do sodas call their father?
Answer: Pop, of course!

Riddle: What made the vegetables go into a panic and call 9!!?
Answer: The arti-choked

Riddle: What fruit do other fruits address as "father?"
Answer: Their papa-ya

Riddle: Why is it a no-no to tell a secret when you are in a farm?
Answer: Because the corn has ears and the potato, eyes

Riddle: What made the banana see the doctor?
Answer: He wasn't peeling well.

Riddle: Why did Mr. and Mrs. Watermelon have a fancy wedding?
Answer: Because they cantaloupe (can't elope)

Riddle: What do grapes do when people step on them?
Answer: They whine (whine).

Riddle: What made the little boy fix his stare at the bottle of orange juice?
Answer: Because the label said "concentrate"

Chapter 2: Christmas and Holidays

Riddle: The animals in the forest wanted to make a musical recording for Christmas. What should the album be called?
Answer: Jungle Bells

Riddle: A Christmas tree was overheard saying something to the Christmas stocking. What did he say?
Answer: "Don't you ever get tired of just hanging around?"

Riddle: What basketball team does Santa root for?
Answer: The NY Old St. Knicks

Riddle: Why did the turkey refuse to eat on Thanksgiving Day?
Answer: It was stuffed.

Riddle: Santa was finding it difficult to walk. He went to the hospital and asked the doctor to give him something to help him walk. Do you know what the doctor gave Santa?
Answer: A candy cane!

Riddle: If a Christmas tree marries an apple, what kind of baby will they have?
Answer: A pine apple.

Riddle: A snowman wanted a snack. What did he get?
Answer: A snow cone!

Riddle: If the year ends with December 31st, how does Christmas end?
Answer: With "s"

Riddle: What laundry detergent should Santa use to wash his clothes with?

Answer: Yule tide

Riddle: What do a snow globe and a water globe feel when it is Christmas?
Answer: A little shaken

Riddle: Who among the reindeer is the most ill-mannered?
Answer: Rude-dolf

Riddle: What made the little drummer boy invite the chickens to join the band?
Answer: Because he saw that they had drum sticks

Riddle: The snowman had dandruff. When he scratched his dry and itchy scalp, what did he see falling?
Answer: Snowflakes!

Riddle: Where do Mr. and Mrs. Claus go for a swim?
Answer: The North Pool.

Riddle: After everybody opens their gifts for Christmas, what do you see?
Answer: A big Christmess

Riddle: What phobia do people who are afraid of Santa Claus suffer from?
Answer: Claustrophobia

Riddle: How can you tell that Santa is in your house for Christmas?
Answer: You sense his presents

Riddle: When Santa spends all his money and is left with nothing, what do you call him?

Answer: St. Nickle-less

Riddle: When an elf has earmuffs on, what do you call him?
Answer: Anything at all. He won't be able to hear you, anyway.

Riddle: What is it about Christmas that Warren Buffet loves most?
Answer: The stock-ings

Riddle: When he was introduced to the most beautiful Christmas lady-angel he had ever seen, what did the gentleman-angel say?
Answer: Halo there, beautiful.

Riddle: What do you call somebody who is related to Santa Claus?
Answer: A relative clause

Riddle: When Mrs. Claus is naughty on Christmas, what does Santa give her?
Answer: A good spanking

Riddle: Santa Claus uses his reindeer and sleigh to travel. The three wise men use a camel. What do the elves use?
Answer: A minivan

Riddle: The terrorists weren't happy with the present they got for Christmas. What did they get?
Answer: A missile-toe

Riddle: What did Mrs. Claus give Santa for Christmas so that he could take pictures wherever he went?
Answer: A Pole-aroid camera

Riddle: When the Christmas bell left the hospital with his medicine, what did he tell his doctor?
Answer: "If I don't feel better after I take this medicine, I'll give you a ring."

Riddle: What crammed the manger full during Christmas?
Answer: The Three Wide Men

Riddle: What did Tom see that made him think that Santa was a werewolf?
Answer: Santa claws

Riddle: What reindeer gets really busy during Valentine's Day?
Answer: Cupid

Riddle: What day of the week are Easter eggs afraid of?
Answer: Fry-days

Riddle: When the day before Christmas came, what did Adam have to say?
Answer: It's Christmas, Eve!

Riddle: Santa made the mistake of going down a chimney which still had fire burning. What happened to Santa?
Answer: He turned into Crisp Kringle!

Riddle: When Christmas is over, where does Santa keep his suit?
Answer: Inside the Claus-et

Riddle: Where do Easter bunnies go for breakfast?
Answer: IHOP

Riddle: Which of Santa's reindeer runs the fastest?
Answer: Dasher

Riddle: Which of Santa's reindeer wants to set off for outer space?
Answer: Comet

Riddle: What do Christmas trees and bad knitters have in common?
Answer: They drop their needles

Riddle: Why did the policeman give Santa a ticket?
Answer: Because Santa parked his sleigh in the Snow Parking Zone
Riddle: What is the only kind of bread that dwarfs and elves eat for Christmas?
Answer: Shortbread.

Chapter 3: It's All in the Family

Riddle: A nurse and a girl went shopping. The girl was the nurse's daughter but the nurse was not the girl's mother. Who was the nurse?
Answer: The girl's father.

Riddle: A girl was brought to the hospital's emergency room. She needed to be operated on. The doctor on duty saw the girl and said: I cannot perform surgery on this girl. She is my daughter. The doctor, however, was not the girl's father. How do you explain this?
Answer: The doctor was her mother.

Riddle: Maureen's mother has 3 daughters. The oldest one is named Sara and the youngest, Cara. What is the name of the middle child?
Answer: Maureen.

Riddle: Aimee's parents have 5 children – Dada, Dede, Didi, Dodo. What is the name of the fifth child?
Answer: No, not Dudu. It is Aimee!

Riddle: Two fathers and two sons go fishing. Each one is able to catch a fish. The total number of fish caught is 3. How do you explain this?
Answer: There were 3 people who went fishing – a grandfather accompanied by his son and grandson.

Riddle: Mrs. Jones has 5 sons. Each of her sons has a sister. How many kids does Mrs. Jones have?
Answer: She has 6 kids. All the sons have the same sister.
Riddle: When the Mrs. Snowman became upset with Mr. Snowman, what did she give him?

Answer: The cold shoulder

Riddle: What did Mr. Baseball Glove say to his wife?
Answer: "Catch you later, honey."

Riddle: Mrs. McNamara has two kids. If the older kid is a girl, what are the odds that Mrs. McNamara's younger kid is also a girl?
Answer: 50%

Riddle: Emily lost her mother in the fair. She looked for her and finally found her in the candied apple stall. What is the first thing that Emily did when she found her mother?
Answer: She stopped looking for her.

Chapter 4: Say That Again, Please?

Riddle: If a wizard from outer space can fly, what kind of wizard is he?
Answer: A flying sorcerer!

Riddle: Billy's mom tested the bath water first before putting Billy in the tub. Why did she do this?
Answer: She didn't want Billy to have son-burn.

Riddle: My name is Max. I stay on a farm with four other dogs. The four dogs are named Brownie, Whitey, Doug, and Spotty. What is the name of the 5th dog?
Answer: Max

Riddle: Harry insisted on carrying his watch to the desert. How do you explain this?
Answer: Harry didn't want to get thirsty. The watch has a spring in it.

Riddle: In what way does a vampire prefer his food served?
Answer: He wants it bite-size.

Riddle: How does a musician clean his dirty tuba?
Answer: He uses a tuba toothpaste!

Riddle: Why did Goldilocks keep on waking up scared in the middle of the night?
Answer: Because she had night bears

Riddle: What do well-mannered ghosts do before entering a house?
Answer: The always wipe their sheets

Riddle: What made the jelly roll?
Answer: Because he wanted to see the apple turn over

Riddle: What kind of music does an angel usually sing in the shower?
Answer: Soul music

Riddle: When you are having an ice-cream sundae with a ghost, what kind of topping do you choose to have?
Answer: Whipped Scream

Riddle: I am not younger than any tree. What kind of tree am I?
Answer: An elder tree

Riddle: What kind of pets like to make stirring classical or jazz music?
Answer: Trum-pets

Riddle: What does the man in the moon like to eat for snacks?
Answer: Space-chips

Riddle: Why was the pony always coughing?
Answer: Because he felt a little horse

Riddle: Where does a butterfly like to sleep?
Answer: On a cater-pillow

Riddle: What is a bumblebee's favorite type of music?
Answer: Bee-Bop

Riddle: After taking a shower, what does a newspaper reporter prefer to use for drying himself up?
Answer: Paper towels

Riddle: What made the court think that the judge was about to go to bed?
Answer: He was already in his robe.

Riddle: When a troll comes home, what does he say to himself?
Answer: It's good to be back in my gnome sweet gnome.

Riddle: What do Mr. and Mrs. Snake's towels have written on them?
Answer: Hiss and Hers

Riddle: Among the witch's friends, who do you think eats really fast?
Answer: The goblin

Riddle: When witches stay in a hotel, what do they usually ask for?
Answer: Broom with a view

Riddle: What part of the newspaper or magazine is a witch usually interested in?
Answer: The horrorscope

Riddle: What did the ghost say to another ghost when they were introduced?
Answer: "How do you boo?"

Riddle: Why did the witches stop in the highway?
Answer: They stopped for the witch-hikers.

Riddle: What country do starving men come from?
Answer: Hungary

Riddle: Why were the tennis players asked to leave the bar?

Answer: Because they were making a racquet

Riddle: Why did the thief steal a deck of cards?
Answer: Because somebody told him it had 13 diamonds

Riddle: When wolves go on vacation, where do they usually check in?
Answer: A howliday inn

Riddle: The sheriff found the thieves sleeping on the ground after they robbed a bank. Why were they doing this?
Answer: The thieves wanted to lie low

Riddle: What is the best name for a camel that has no hump?
Answer: Humphrey

Riddle: In summer, what do frogs like to wear on the beach?
Answer: Open toad sandals

Riddle: Where does a pilot prefer to keep his personal belongings?
Answer: In air pockets

Riddle: What do astronauts and prisoners have in common?
Answer: They both would like to be sent to outer space

Riddle: What happens when a clock gets together with a dog?
Answer: There will be more than enough tics to go around.

Riddle: How did the hikers get to be with the poison ivy?
Answer: They itch hiked.

Riddle: How does a cow who owns a store count his earnings?
Answer: He uses a 'cow'nter.

Riddle: What dish did the cook come up when he cooked beef and chicken together?
Answer: Roost beef

Riddle: How does the delivery boy deliver pizza?
Answer: On a pie-cycle

Riddle: Why was Miss Cow scared?
Answer: Because her boyfriend got into a bullfight!

Riddle: Why did the river flood?
Answer: Because it got too big for her bridges

Riddle: What happens when a cement truck runs into a prison?
Answer: You get hardened criminals.

Riddle: How did the baby robot let his mom know that he loved her?
Answer: He hugged her and told her, "I wuv you, mama – watts and watts!"

Riddle: At what time do tooth fairies visit kids to exchange a tooth for a dollar?
Answer: A tooth o'clock

Riddle: Why did the geeks want to see the doctor?
Answer: Because they wanted him to give them an Apple a day

Riddle: Crayons go to Color-ado for the holidays. The cats go to Kat-zakhstan. Where do dogs spend the holidays?
Answer: In Paw-land

Riddle: What made Mrs. Pig leave her husband?
Answer: She found him to be a terrible boar.

Riddle: Why was the geologist's wife so miserable?
Answer: Because she felt that he was taking her for granite

Riddle: What does a goblin usually sing when he is in the shower?
Answer: Rhythm and boos

Riddle: Tom is a plumber. What is his favorite song?
Answer: "Singing in the Drain"

Riddle: Sheep like to eat this type of chocolate. What is it?
Answer: A Hersheys baaa

Riddle: What is the part of the ocean that kindles romance?
Answer: The place where buoy meets gull

Riddle: What is a snowman's favorite breakfast fare?
Answer: Snowflakes

Riddle: When a pumpkin falls from your basket, what do you get?
Answer: Squash

Riddle: What does a cheerleader eat for breakfast?
Answer: Cheerios

Riddle: What meal does an astronaut enjoy the most?
Answer: Launch

Riddle: What happens when an Indian potato changes its nationality?
Answer: He turns into French fries.

Riddle: What does a basketball player do with a donut?
Answer: He dunks it.

Riddle: Why did the teacher instruct the children not to tell jokes to the Easter egg?
Answer: Because the Easter egg might crack up

Riddle: When a girl fell down the ladder, her brother couldn't help her. How do you explain this?
Answer: He couldn't be a brother and, at the same time, assist her (a sister).

Riddle: Why was grandma excited about sitting down on the rocking chair and wearing her roller blades at the same time?
Answer: Because she was excited to rock and roll

Riddle: When the boy cat finally met the love of his life, what did he tell her?
Answer: You are just purrr-fect for me!

Riddle: If you want to drink the healthy water, what type of water should you take?
Answer: Well water

Riddle: Who usually wins in a beauty contest for skeletons?
Answer: No body

Riddle: What flowers do girl squirrels receive on Valentine's Day?
Answer: Forget-me-nuts

Riddle: How do you describe a weather that is raining turkeys?
Answer: Fowl weather

Riddle: Why does the Easter Rabbit like the fairy tale Cinderella so much?
Answer: Because it has a hoppy ending!

Riddle: Why should you keep from ironing a four-leaf clover?
Answer: Because you wouldn't want to press your luck

Riddle: What did Judge Mason whisper to the Pillsbury Doughboy?
Answer: Please rise.

Riddle: When the waiter brought the bill after the duck had lunch in the restaurant, what did the duck say?
Answer: No, thank you. I already have one (a bill).

Riddle: What snack do school children take when they have their mid-morning break in school?
Answer: Reese's (recess)

Riddle: What do cowboys who ride wild horses often get sick of?
Answer: Bronco-itis

Riddle: What made the baker quit baking doughnuts?
Answer: He got fed up with the hole business.

Riddle: Why did the policeman arrest the belt?
Answer: Because the belt held up the pants

Riddle: What made the cookie consult the doctor?
Answer: He felt crumbly.

Riddle: What did the leopard say after he had a good lunch?
Answer: "Why, that certainly hit the spot!"

Riddle: What did one plate tell the other plate when they got together for dinner?
Answer: "The dinner is on me."

Riddle: What made the tomato blush?
Answer: He came into the room in time to see the salad dressing.

Riddle: What did Mama Knife say to Papa Knife?
Answer: "Be sharp!"

Riddle: When the bad guys entered the room, they found Superman wrapping himself in bread. Why?
Answer: Because he wanted a hero sandwich!

Riddle: When should you run from a clock?
 Answer: When it is time for the clock to run down and strike

Riddle: Why couldn't the soldier who brought a camouflage sleeping bag with him sleep?
Answer: Because he couldn't find his sleeping bag

Riddle: What do a dull axe and coffee have in common?
Answer: You need to ground them before you use them.

Riddle: How does a glutton differ from a hungry man?
A glutton eats too long while a hungry man longs to eat.

Riddle: What do annoying guests and trees in winter have in common?
Answer: They both take too long to leave.

Riddle: How do you go about fixing a pizza?
Answer: Just use tomato paste

Riddle: What is a cannibal's favorite pizza?
Answer: A pizza that has everyone in it

Riddle: Why is chocolate not allowed in jail?
Answer: Because it causes you to break out

Riddle: Why did the police arrest the cook?
Answer: They found him whipping the cream and beating the eggs.

Riddle: A cake was flirting with the fork. What did she say to him?
Answer: "Hey, handsome! You want a piece of me, don't you?"

Riddle: What made the little girl put a piece of candy underneath her pillow?
Answer: She wanted to have sweet dreams.

Riddle: What do breads do after you bake them?
Answer: They just loaf around.

Riddle: What happened to the Italian chef who had terminal cancer?
Answer: He pasta-way.

Riddle: What does a cab driver wear if he goes to a ball?
Answer: A taxi-do

Riddle: Why did Mama Elf send Baby Elf to school?
Answer: So he could learn his elf-abet.

Riddle: What happens when an ax falls on the car that you are driving?
Answer: You have an ax-ident.

Riddle: What happens to a boy who eats Christmas décor?
Answer: He gets tinsel-itis.

Riddle: Why did the runner go to school?
Answer: Because he wanted to learn Jog-raphy

Riddle: What game do sheep play when they get together?
Answer: Baa-dminton

Riddle: If you ate cheese that didn't belong to you, what kind of cheese would you have eaten?
Answer: Nacho cheese!

Riddle: What kind of music is played in space?
Answer: A nept-tune

Riddle: If you are flossing your teeth and broke a tooth, what would you do?
Answer: Get a tooth paste.

Riddle: What does a frying pan and Europe have in common?
Answer: They both have grease (Greece) at the bottom.

Riddle: When two witches live together in one room, what do you call them?
Answer: Broommates!

Riddle: If you want to become invisible, what should you drink?
Answer: Evaporated milk

Riddle: What did the beach tell the tide when it came in?
Answer: "Long time, no sea!"

Riddle: What do you call a situation when hamsters are caught in traffic and can't move at all?
Answer: A hamsterjam

Riddle: Why did the potato chips go to the beach?
Answer: Because they wanted to go for a dip

Riddle: Why did the sailors stop playing cards?
Answer: Because they saw the captain on the deck

Riddle: If a bull charges a person, what should that person do?
Answer: Pay the bull

Riddle: Why doesn't anyone want to play basketball with a pig?
Answer: Because the pig always hogs the ball

Riddle: When does a car stop being a car?
Answer: The moment it turns into a parking lot

Riddle: Who is considered the faster runner of all times?
Answer: Adam. He came first in the human race.

Riddle: Why did the hot dog refuse to star in the movie?
Answer: He didn't like the roll he was offered.

Riddle: Why did the criminal hold up the bakeshop?
Answer: He "kneaded" the "dough."

Riddle: I am a vegetable. I am the last thing you want to be in a ship with you. What am I?

Answer: A "leek"

Riddle: What do you do to have sheep in ink?
Answer: You use a pen to draw them!

Riddle: What made the sheriff attend the barbeque?
Answer: He thought it was the best place for a "steak" out.

Riddle: What is likely to happen when a sea monster has a tantrum?
Answer: You will see a "comm-ocean."

Riddle: What happens when a hen marries a guitar?
Answer: They give birth to a chicken who can pluck itself.

Riddle: What kind of songs does a father sing when he gets in the shower?
Answer: Pop songs

Riddle: How did the handyman fix the robot gorilla?
Answer: He used a monkey wrench.

Riddle: What does an elf do after school?
Answer: Gnomework!

Riddle: What kind of chin is never shaved?
Answer: A sea urchin

Riddle: How did Emma make the strawberry shake?
Answer: She told it a scary story!

Riddle: I am a famous nurse. People know me for wearing my pajamas when I work. Who am I?
Answer: Florence Nightingown

Riddle: When does a man become sour?
Answer: When he gets in a pickle

Riddle: What do a naughty boy and a dirty rug have in common?

Answer: Both of them need beating.

Riddle: What do a bruise and a bubble have in common?
Answer: They both come from a blow.

Riddle: Tell me the kind of money that vampires prefer to use.
Answer: Blood money

Riddle: What does Sir Lancelot prefer to wear in bed?
Answer: A knight gown!

Riddle: Why aren't artists chosen to join sports matches?
Answer: Because they always draw

Riddle: Why am I wearing a helmet to dinner?
Answer: Because I am on a crash diet

Riddle: Tom made a sandwich but it sank to bottom of the tub
before he could eat it. What kind of sandwich did Tom make?
Answer: A submarine sandwich!

Riddle: What is the name of the fairy that refuses to take baths?
Answer: Stinker Bell.

Riddle: What happens when you step on a banana peel? You slip
and fall.
What happens when you step on an orange? You get in a jam.
What happens when you step on blueberries? You feel blue.
What happens when you step on grapes?
Answer: You get wine.

Riddle: What happens when a vampire dates a teacher?
Answer: You get a lot of blood tests!

Riddle: What do you call a fake stone if you find it in Ireland?

Answer: A Shamrock.

Riddle: What position does a ghost play when he plays soccer?
Answer: Ghoul keeper

Riddle: Why is orange juice always on the top of his class?
Answer: Because it concentrates.

Riddle: What made Dr. Scientist mount a knocker on the door?
Answer: Because he was bent on getting a No-bell prize!

Riddle: Why did they suspend Cinderella from the basketball team?
Answer: Because she wanted to leave the ball.

Chapter 5: Stories – Go Figure

Riddle: A farmer went to town with a goose, a fox, and a sack of corn. He came up to a brook. He saw a tiny boat which he could use to cross the brook. However, he could only bring one thing at a time when he crossed.
If he leaves the fox behind, it would eat the goose. If he left the goose with the sack of corn, it would eat the corn. What did the farmer do to get all of them safely across the brook?
Answer: The farmer brought the goose with him over to the other side of the brook first and came back. Then he took the fox over to other side but brought back the goose with him. Leaving the goose, he then took the sack of corn over to the other side. He came back to carry the goose over.

Riddle: A man drove a black car. All his lights failed; he could not use any of them. The moon wasn't out to give light either. A child crossed the street. The man immediately stopped his car to let the child cross safely. How did the man spot the child crossing?
Answer: The sun was shining. It was a beautiful day.

Riddle: In a beautiful one-storey yellow cottage, there lived a yellow person with a yellow cat who had a yellow bow. He had yellow fish which he kept in a yellow fish tank. He worked on a yellow computer on his yellow desk. He had a yellow chair, a yellow telephone, and a yellow bath tub. Everything in that cottage was yellow.
What color were the stairs?
Answer: There were no stairs. It was a one-storey cottage.

Riddle: A man sits in a house at night without a single light. He has no candle, no flashlight, and no lamp. Nevertheless, he is reading. How does he do it?
 Answer: Being blind, he reads Braille.

Riddle: A man walks into a house at night and finds a fireplace, a kerosene lamp, and a candle. What does he light first?
Answer: A match

Riddle: Two mothers and two daughters went out for a snack. Each one had one burger but somehow only 3 burgers were consumed in all? How do you explain this?
Answer: The women were a daughter, mother, and grandma

Riddle: A man took a walk. It rained. The man didn't have a hat or an umbrella. His clothes got soaking wet. However, not a single strand of hair on his head became even a bit damp. How did this happen?
Answer: This man had no hair; he was bald.

Riddle: A cowboy rode into our town on Monday. He stayed for a couple of days. He left town on Monday. How was did possible?
Answer: The cowboy rode into town on a horse named Monday.

Riddle: You have two pails -- a 3-gallon pail and a 5-gallon pail. You have access to as much water as you want. Using no other measuring device, what do you do to fill the 5-gallon pail with precisely four gallons of water?
Answer: Fill the 5-gallon pail to the brim. Pour water from this pail into the 3-gallon pail to fill it to the brim. Pour out the water from the 3-gallon pail. Refill the 3-gallon pail with the remaining 2 gallons from the 5-gallon pail. Fill the 5-gallon pail to the brim again. Transfer water to the 3-gallon pail until it is full. You now have exactly 4 gallons of water in the 5-gallon pail.

Riddle: An electric train runs at 60 miles an hour heading towards the east. It runs through a powerful westerly wind. In what direction will the train's smoke go?
Answer: The electric train has no smoke.

Riddle: Imagine that you are imprisoned in a dark room that has no doors or windows. The room fills with water fast. How will you escape?
Answer: You simply stop imagining.

Riddle: Mr. Jones lives in a palatial circular home. One day, he noticed an ugly dark strawberry jam stain on his beautiful and expensive new carpet. He asked around to find out which of the people at home was responsible for the stain.
Everybody had excuses: The chef said that he was busy preparing lunch in the kitchen. Billy said that he was playing basketball outside. The maid said that she was busy polishing the corners of the house. Who was lying?
Answer: The maid couldn't have been polishing the corners of the house. The house being circular had no corners.

Riddle: You open a room and find Romeo and Juliet lifeless on the floor. You find water and several broken pieces of glass near them. You look around and can see only a bed and shelf.
There are no houses nearby. There is only a railroad track.
How did Romeo and Juliet die?
Answer: Romeo and Juliet are goldfish. When the train passed by, it made a big rumble. The vibration caused the fishbowl to fall off the shelf. The bowl broke. Both Romeo and Juliet die.

Riddle: Twenty people stand in a square room. The room is empty except for these 20 people. There is no furniture. There are no décor. Each individual in the room, by moving his eyes, can see the entire room. He doesn't even have to turn his body or head.

Where do you put a bright red box so that everybody, except one individual, can see it?
Answer: You put the box on that individual's head.

Riddle: At a carnival, a boy approached a man and said: "Will you pay me $100 if I am able to write your exact weight on this piece of paper? If I fail to do that, I will give you $200."
The man couldn't see any weighing scale around. Thinking that he would just say that he weighed more or less than what the boy would write on the paper, he agreed.
The story ends with the man paying the boy $100. How do you explain this?
Answer: The man opened the piece of paper after the boy wrote on it. The paper read. "your exact weight."

Riddle: Alice and her younger sister, Jill, were fighting. Their mother got fed up with them and punished them. She made them stand on a newspaper. Alice and Jill stood on the same newspaper but they couldn't even touch each other. How did this happen??
Answer: Their mother slid the newspaper under the bedroom door. Alice stayed on one side of the closed door; Jill stood on the other side.

Riddle: In a contest, all the contestants were asked to hold something. The winner was someone who had no feet or hands. How can this be?
Answer: The contestants were asked to hold their breath.

Riddle: A man lived in a place where it is summer for 6 months of the year and winter in the remaining months. He owns a lake and a small island across it.
The man wants to build a house on the island. However, he does not own a boat, a plane, or any transportation which he can use

to bring the materials he needs to the island. However, he was able to build the house he wanted. How did he do it?
Answer: He waited for winter. The lake froze and he was able to bring everything he needed to build the house across the lake.

Riddle: A boy was asked to choose between an old one-hundred dollar bill and a new one. The boy chose the older bill. Why?
Answer: The boy chose the older $100 bill because it was worth more than a new one ($1).

Riddle: A policemen saw Al, a truck driver, going against the traffic on a one-way street. The policeman simply waved at Al and went his way. He didn't arrest or stop Al. How do you explain this?
Answer: Al was walking down the street.

Riddle: Tom is a very rich guy. He looks around for a used car to buy. He finally finds a gorgeous Buick which sells for $10,000. Tom buys the Buick and he does so without paying a dime. How do you explain this?
Answer: Tom pays the $10,000 but he didn't include any dime when he paid.

Riddle: A four o'clock in the morning, John hears someone knocking on the door. Without leaving his bedroom, he quickly asks "Who is there?" and hears his parents' reply. They are there to have breakfast with John.
John becomes a bit flustered and quickly thinks about what food he has in the pantry. He has eggs, bread, butter, and jam. What should John open first?
Answer: The door.

Riddle: Sam was on his way to Mayfair. He comes face to face with a man with 7 wives. Each wife was carrying 7 rucksacks.

Each rucksack contained 7 cats, with each cat nursing 7 kittens.
How many were on their way to Mayfair?
Answer: Only 1, Sam.

Riddle: Val, a bus driver, and Sal, a surgeon, are wooing the
same woman Gal.
Val has to leave for 7 days to drive the bus. He came to visit Gal
the day before he left to give her 10 apples. How do you explain
this?
Answer: Val believes that a daily dose of apple (an apple a day)
will keep Sal (the doctor) away.

Riddle: Paul puts a coin inside a wine bottle. He then puts a cork
in the wine bottle. An hour later, he takes the coin out of the
wine bottle. He does this without having to take the cork out or
having to break the wine bottle. How do you explain this?
Answer: John pushed the cork inside the wine bottle.

Riddle: There are two rows of glasses. Each row has three
glasses each. The glasses in the first row contain milk. The
glasses in the second row are empty.
I move only one glass and the empty and full glasses in each row
now alternate. How do you explain this?
Answer: I take the middle glass in the row of milk-filled glasses
and pour the milk into the middle glass in the row of empty
glasses.

Riddle: You come into the bathroom and find the bathtub filled
to the brim with water. You have a cup, a teaspoon, and a
tablespoon. What is the quickest way to get rid of the water?
Answer: Simply drain the water like you always do.

Riddle: Emma went at red and stopped at green. How do you
explain this?

Answer: She was eating a watermelon.

Riddle: You are sentenced to prison. But you get to choose what room to stay in. One room is filled with murderers who have knives. Another room is packed with mad people who have guns. The last one is crammed with wolves that have not eaten for three years. What room would you choose?
Answer: The last one. Wolves that don't eat for three years are dead.

Riddle: Albert is lost in the woods where there is no plumbing, ventilation, or electricity. A ferocious tiger is running after him. Albert needs to hide from the tiger. He comes to a creepy house with 3 rooms. The 1st room has a famished lion in it. The 2nd room has a crazy knife-wielding criminal. The 3rd room has an electric chair. Albert has to quickly choose a room to escape from the tiger. Which room should he pick?
Answer: The 3rd room. The electric chair doesn't work because there is no electricity.

Riddle: Alan was on the 18th floor of a building cleaning the windows on an office block. The electricity suddenly went off. Alan could not use the electric hoist that supported his platform. How did Alan get down to the ground before the electricity came on again?
Answer: Alan simply used the stairs. He was inside the building cleaning the interior part of the windows.

Riddle: Angelina, Brad, John, Stella, Tom, Cookie, Teresa, Joseph, Jan, Claire, and Aimee were passengers in an airplane. The airplane crashed and every single passenger on board died. When the ambulance arrived on the scene, Brad and Angelina were still alive. How do you explain this?
Answer: Brad and Angelina are married. They are not single.

Riddle: It was raining really hard. The little rabbit stayed out playing for hours in the rain. When he went home, he didn't have a single strand of wet hair. How do you explain this?
Riddle: The rabbit had fur. He didn't have hair.

Riddle: A beautiful orange and yellow dead butterfly is caught in a huge spider web. The spider sees it and comes running to eat it. What should the butterfly do to escape from the spider: wiggle its legs, flutter its wings, or both?
Answer: It is too late for the butterfly to do anything. It is already dead.

Riddle: A queen gave birth to twins by Caesarian section so they couldn't tell who was the older of the twins. One of the twins grew up to be charismatic, well-loved by the people, and very intelligent. The other was stupid.
The time came for one of the children to take over the throne. The stupid one became the ruler. How do you explain this?
Answer: The stupid one was male. The other child was female.

Riddle: Anna, Adelaide, and Gertrude are triplets. But Anna and Adelaide have something that Gertrude does not. What is this?
Answer: The letter 'A' in her name.

Riddle: Farmer Sam brought some watermelons from his farm to sell in the market. He was able to sell half of them in addition to half a watermelon. He was left with one unsold watermelon. How many watermelons did he bring from his farm?
Answer: 3

Riddle: Five men were on their way to church. It began to rain. Four men ran to seek cover. One man stayed behind. The four men got wet. The one who remained stayed dry. How do you explain this?

Answer: The 4 men were pallbearers. The man who remained dry was the dead man inside the coffin.

Riddle: John sits in his cabin in Texas. After 3 hours, he gets out of his cabin and finds that he is in Michigan. How do you explain this?
Answer: John is a pilot. He was staying in the pilot's cabin in an airplane.

Riddle: There are three oranges in the basket. Aimee, Claire, and Maureen took home one orange each. How is it that there was still an orange in the basket?
Answer: Maureen took home her orange in the basket.

Riddle: Why did the worried girl say "yes" when the doctor asked her if she was getting enough iron?
Answer: Because she always chewed her nails

Chapter 6: Numbers and Words

Riddle: I am a number – an odd number. However, if you remove one letter, I become even. Who am I?
Answer: Seven (remove "s" from "seven" and you are left with "even")

Riddle: How do you use addition to get 1000 out of eight 8s?
Answer: 8 + 88 + 8 + 888 + 8 = 1000

Riddle: Little Tummy Tucker took two turtles and tied them to two tall trees using two strong strings. How many T's in that?
Answer: T-h-a-t has 2 T's

Riddle: You see 10 blackbirds sitting on a fence. You got your gun and shoot one. How many blackbirds do you now see on the fence?
Answer: None. Each one would have flown away upon hearing the shot.

Riddle: You see 2 ducks swimming in front of a duck, a duck swimming in the middle, and 2 ducks swimming behind a duck. How many ducks do you see?
Answer: Three

Riddle: There were 12 pears hanging on a tree. Twelve men passed by. Each took a pear and ate it. There were 11 pears left hanging on the tree. How do you explain this?
Answer: The man who took a pear was named Each.

Riddle: I own a money box that measures 48 square centimeters. It is 42 centimeters in height. How many coins can I fit into my empty box?

Answer: You can put in only one coin. After that, the money box is no longer empty.

Riddle: We are 3 positive numbers. You get the same answer whether you add or multiply us. What are we?
Answer: The numbers 1, 2, 3

Riddle: You see 7 ripe mangoes in a basket. Without asking for permission, you immediately take 3 mangoes. How many mangoes do you have?
Answer: 3, of course!

Riddle: Bill turns twenty on his birthday. However, he has celebrated only 5 birthdays. How do you explain this?
Answer: Bill was born on a leap year.

Riddle: Henry gets a telephone's number pad and multiplies all the numbers on it. What number does he get?
Answer: 0

Riddle: If you are holding 3 mangoes and 4 apples in your right hand and 4 oranges and 3 apples in your left, what do you have?
Answer: Extremely large hands

Riddle: Joe finds 3 stoves in the cabin he is renting – a brick stove, a glass stove, and a wooden stove. He only has 1 match. What should Joe light up first?
Answer: The match

Riddle: A family of five is having apple pie for dessert. The pie is cut into five slices. Each member of the family has a slice of pie in front of him. However, one slice of pie is still in the pie tin. How do you explain this?
Answer: One of them is getting his slice of pie in the pie tin.

Riddle: It takes 20 men 5 hours to build a certain wall. How many hours will 10 men need to put up this same wall?
Answer: They need no time at all. The wall has already been built.

Riddle: A big number of your friends come to visit you. After an hour, they get thirsty and ask for water. The first one asks for ¼ cup of water. The second one asks for 1/8 cup of water. The third one asks for ½ cup of water, etc. How many cups of water do you have to have so you can give your friends what they want?
Answer: You only need one cup to measure out the amount of water that they are asking for.

Riddle: Use half of five to make four.
Answer: FIVE is spelled with 4 letters. Take away half of that by removing the letters "F" and "E." What remains is IV – the Roman numeral for four.

Riddle: How many bricks do you need in order to finish a house made of bricks?
Answer: One. Add the last brick and you're done.

Riddle: It takes two men four days to make a hole. How long will one man take to make half a hole?
Answer: There is no half a hole.

Riddle: I have 18 goats. After a really bad storm, all but 10 goats die. How many living goats do I still have?
Answer: 10!

Riddle: Why are 1983 10-pound notes worth less than 1998 10-pound notes?
Answer: Because there are fewer notes!

Riddle: A group of soldiers were being drilled under the blistering sun. They were all facing north.
The sergeant barked out his instructions: Left turn! About turn! Right turn! Guess in what direction the soldiers are now facing.
Answer: South. The soldiers turned 90 degrees to make a left turn. They turned 180 degrees to make an about turn. Then they took another 90 degrees to make a right turn. They now face south.

Riddle: In what length do ladies usually wear their skirts?
Answer: Above their two feet

Riddle: Two girls played chess. They played 7 games. Each girl won 7 times. How do you explain this?
Answer: The two girls weren't playing with each other.

Riddle: How many plates can you set on an empty table?
Answer: Only one. Once you put that on the table, the table is no longer empty.

Riddle: John has two coins, one of which is not a dime. The two coins total 35 cents. What two coins does John have?
Answer: A dime and a quarter. One coin (the quarter) is not a dime.

Riddle: There are three oranges in the basket. You take two oranges. How many do you have?
Answer: You have two oranges, of course.

Riddle: What do the numbers 88, 69, and 11 have in common?
Answer: All numbers read the same upside down and right side up.

Riddle: Three men were on a ship. The ship capsized. Only 2 men got their hair wet. Why is this so?

Answer: One man was bald.

Riddle: You have 3 matches. Without breaking any of them, how do you make the 3 matches 4?
Answer: You simply get the 3 matches to form the Roman numeral IV.

Riddle: You see 6 rubber ducks floating in the pond. Three floated away. Two sank. How many of the ducks remain alive?
Answer: Zero. Rubber ducks are toys; they are not alive.

Riddle: What is the 5-letter word that contains a thousand letters?
Answer: Bible

Riddle: What does "I right I" mean?
Answer: It means right between the eyes.

Riddle: You make this 5-letter word even shorter by adding 2 letters to it. What word is it?
Answer: Short

Riddle: The sign read, "Look out for cars, Railroad crossing." How do you spell that without using the letter "r?"
Answer: t-h-a-t

Riddle: I begin the end. I end every place. Eternity starts with me. Both time and space end with me. What am I?
Answer: The letter "e"

Riddle: Spell "candy" using only 2 letters.
Answer: c and y – with the spaces removed

Riddle: When you remove the whole, you are still left with some. What is it?

Answer: The word "wholesome"

Riddle: Spell COW using 13 letters.
Answer: S E E – O - DOUBLE YOU

Riddle: Children Playing – Go Slow. Spell that with no letter "L."
Answer: T-H-A-T

Riddle: What do you call a bear without ear?
Answer: 'B'

Riddle: I run fast. People spell me the same way frontwards and backwards. What am I?
Answer: Racecar

Riddle: I am a word made out of five letters. However, even if you take out 3 letters – the first, the one in the middle, and the last one, I don't sound different. What am I?
Answer: The word EMPTY

Riddle: How do you spell "enemy" using only 3 letters?
Answer: F O E

Riddle: The queen bee buzzed. The honey bee buzzed. The worker bee buzzed. The killer bee buzzed. There was a lot of buzzing going on. Tell me how many bees there are in buzzing.
Answer: One. Buzzing only has one b.

Riddle: What comes just once in a minute, two times in a moment, and never in a hundred years?
Answer: The letter M

Riddle: Make these words into a sentence that makes sense. Do not change the order of the words. Use the following punctuation marks only: 1 question mark and 3 periods.

That that is is that that is not is not is that it it is
Answer: "That that is is that that is. Not is not. Is that it? It is."
Or: "That that is is. That that is not is not. Is that it? It is."

Chapter 7: Short and Sometimes Not So Simple

Riddle: How many women were born in 2001?
Answer: None. Only babies were born

Riddle: You drive a bus. Three kids get on the bus as two kids get off. In the next block, three get off and two get on. In the next block, eight kids get off, as four kids get on.
What is the color of the driver's eyes?
Answer: Look at your eyes to get the answer; you drive the bus, after all.

Riddle: Why do eggs refrain from telling jokes?
Answer: Because they don't like to make each other crack up

Riddle: I am a pretty cool tick. I am either white or black. I can be found in clothes and shoes. What am I?
Answer: The Nike logo

Riddle: I have teeth but I don't use them to eat. What am I?

Answer: A comb

Riddle: What is the easiest way to make milk shake?
Answer: Scare it with a "Boo!"

Riddle: What question is always answered with a "yes?"
Answer: "Y" "E" "S" – how do you read that?

Riddle: What comes with hands but can't clap?
Answer: A clock

Riddle: What lies at the rainbow's end?

Answer: The letter W

Riddle: What begins with "t," gets filled with "t," and finishes with "t?"
Answer: A teapot

Riddle: A girl drew a line. Without touching this line, she makes it a longer line. How did she do it?
Answer: She drew a 2nd line (a shorter one) next to it. This made the 1st line she drew longer – even if she did not touch it.

Riddle: What weighs less, a pound of chicken or a pound of chicken feathers?
Answer: Both of them weigh the same

Riddle: Which one of the 12 months in a year has 28 days?
Answer: All of them

Riddle: What 4 days begin with the letter "t?"
Answer: Today, Tomorrow, Tuesday, and Thursday

Riddle: What circles the wood, going round and round it, but never goes into it?
Answer: The tree bark

Riddle: What thing is able to hold water even if it is full of holes?
Answer: A sponge

Riddle: How do you throw a ball with all your strength and find it coming back to you without bouncing off anything?
Answer: You simply hurl the ball up into the air.

Riddle: How do you pay a dog catcher?
Answer: By the pound

Riddle: I never ask questions. However, people usually answer me. What am I?
Answer: A doorbell

Riddle: If you eat me, you die. Rich people need me. Poor people have me. What am I?
Answer: Nothing

Riddle: I have a lot of keys. However, I can't open doors. What am I?
Answer: A piano

Riddle: The person who made me doesn't want me. The one who bought me doesn't need me. The one who used me didn't see me. What am I?
Answer: A coffin

Riddle: I have no arms. I have no legs. But I have 2 hands and a face. What am I?
Answer: A clock

Riddle: I keep going up. I never come down. What am I?
Answer: Your age

Riddle: Without including Monday, Wednesday, and Friday, mention three consecutive days.
Answer: Yesterday, today, tomorrow

Riddle: I am a coat. But you can only put me on when I am wet. What am I?
Answer: Coat of paint

Riddle: I run but I never walk. I murmur but I never talk. I have a bed but I never sleep. I have a mouth but I never eat. What am I?
Answer: A river

Riddle: I become sharper the more you use me. What am I?
Answer: Your brain

Riddle: If you refuse to share me, you keep me. The moment you share me, I cease to be. What am I?
Answer: A secret

Riddle: You can't throw me but you can catch me. What am I?
Answer: A cold

Riddle: I come out at night without you calling me. You lose me during the day although nobody steals me. What am I?
Answer: A star

Riddle: Two behind, one in the middle, and two in front. How many are there?
Answer: three 1 (2 3) - 1 (2) 3 - (1 2) 3

Riddle: I begin and end with the letter "E" but I only have one letter. What am I?
Answer: A letter envelope

Riddle: I am a kind of cheese that is made backwards. What am I?
Answer: Edam

Riddle: I begin with the letter "P," end with the letter "E," and have much more than a thousand letters. What am I?
Answer: The Post Office

Riddle: When can you say that a door is not really a door?
Answer: When it is a jar.

Riddle: In this sequence JFMAMJJASON, what letter comes next?
Answer: "D" for December

Riddle: I have 4 legs but I can't walk. What am I?
Answer: A table

Riddle: Can you make the number one disappear? How?
Answer: You simply put the letter "G" before it and "one" is "gone!"

Riddle: What do an island and the letter "t" have in common?
Answer: They are both in the middle of water

Riddle: My pants pocket is empty. But I have something in it. How do you explain this?
Answer: I have a hole in my pocket.

Riddle: A Teddy bear is never hungry. Why is this so?
Answer: Because he is always stuffed

Riddle: How did the chewing gum woo the shoe?
Answer: He said, "I am stuck on you."

Riddle: What is a joke book on eggs called?
Answer: A yolk book

Riddle: What is the fail-safe cure for dandruff?
Answer: Baldness

Riddle: What will an outlaw get when he steals a calendar?
Answer: 12 months

Riddle: Supercalifragilisticexpialidocious – how do you spell that?
Answer: T-H-A-T

Riddle: What kind of a bank doesn't have any money?
Answer: A riverbank

Riddle: I have no fingers but I have many rings. What am I?
Answer: A telephone

Riddle: There are only two things that I can't have for breakfast. What are these?
Answer: Lunch and dinner

Riddle: What is the longest word you can find in the dictionary?
Answer: Smiles – a full mile separates the two "s's"

Riddle: Mr. Black lives in the black house. Mr. Violet lives in the violet house. Mr. Red lives in the red house. Who lives in the white house?
Answer: The President

Riddle: A judge, a doctor, and a mayor walked down the street. Who wore the biggest hat?
Answer: He who had the biggest head

Riddle: When I am down, I can go up the chimney. When I am up, however, I can never go down the chimney. What am I?
Answer: An umbrella

Riddle: You have to break me before you can use me. What am I?
Answer: An egg

Riddle: In the alphabet, what letter contains the most water?
Answer: C

Riddle: I have existed for millions of years. However, I am no older than a month. What am I?
Answer: The moon

Riddle: I have a bottom on top of me. What am I?
Answer: My legs

Riddle: You always put me on the table to cut but you never eat me. What am I?
Answer: A deck of card

Riddle: These are stones that you never find at sea. What are these?
Answer: Dry stones

Riddle: I become larger even as you remove more from me. What am I?
Answer: A hole

Riddle: I have my head at night but I lose it in the morning. What am I?
Answer: A pillow

Riddle: I am round on both ends and high in the middle. What am I?
Answer: Ohio

Riddle: I break when nobody holds me. What am I?
Answer: A promise

Riddle: I am always coming. I never arrive. What am I?
Answer: Tomorrow

Riddle: I have 88 keys but I can't even get one door open. What am I?
Answer: A piano

Riddle: I have an eye. But I can't see. What am I?
Answer: A needle

Riddle: I have four eyes but can't see. What am I?
Answer: Mississippi

Riddle: I stay only in one spot. However, I have traveled all over the world. What am I?
Answer: A stamp

Riddle: You whip me. You beat me. But I never cry. What am I?
Answer: An egg

Riddle: I may have a hundred limbs yet I can't walk. What am I?
Answer: A tree

Riddle: I always get served. However, no one eats me. What am I?
Answer: A tennis ball.

Riddle: I fly around the entire day but I never get anywhere. What am I?
Answer: A flag

Riddle: I go up and down but I stay in one place. What am I?

Answer: The stairs

Riddle: I don't wear pants but I do wear a jacket. What am I?
Answer: A book

Riddle: I have a bark but don't have a bite. What am I?
Answer: A tree

Riddle: I don't have a head. But I have a neck. I also wear a cap. What am I?
Answer: A bottle

Riddle: What comes with six legs, four eyes, two heads, and a tail?
Answer: A cowboy on his horse

Riddle: In what kind of building can you find the most stories?
Answer: A library.
Riddle: Even when I go off, I stay where I am. What am I?
Answer: An alarm clock

Riddle: I run, yet I have no feet. I point, yet I have no fingers. I strike, yet I have no arms. What am I?
Answer: A clock

Riddle: Thirty men are we, with two women who have more power than all. Clad in black and white, we fight till we fall. What are we?
Answer: Chess pieces

Riddle: Even if they almost die of hunger, the people living in the Arctic find it difficult to eat penguins. How do you explain this?
Answer: You will find it difficult to find a penguin in the Arctic. Penguins are found in the Antarctic.

Riddle: How many lemons grow on a tree?
Answer: All lemons grow on trees.

Riddle: I run around your home – and I don't even move. What am I?
Answer: A fence

Riddle: I have 2 books. I turn the first book upside down. I rotate the second book so that the top of the book faces me. I take the first page number of the first book and add that to the first page number of the second book. What sum do I get?
Answer: 2. 1 + 1 = 2. A book will always have 1 as its first page regardless of how the book is oriented.

Riddle: When you take more, you leave more. What is it?
Answer: Footsteps.

Riddle: I can only point in a single direction. However, I help people find their way all over the world. What am I?
Answer: Compass

Riddle: I build gold crowns and silver bridges. What am I?
Answer: A dentist

Riddle: Drop me from the top of the highest building and I will survive. However, drop me from the tiniest boat and I won't. What am I?
Answer: Paper

Riddle: Chicken or egg - can you guess what comes first?
Answer: Chicken always comes before egg in the dictionary.

Riddle: What is it that you own that others use more than you do?
Answer: Your name

Riddle: What ancient invention makes you see right through walls?

Answer: Windows

Riddle: Scientists have always debated about what stands between heaven and earth. Can you guess?
Answer: "and"

Riddle: I become harder to catch the harder you run. What am I?
Answer: Your breath.

Riddle: If you were an astronaut, at what time would you eat your sandwich?
Answer: At launch time

Riddle: At what point does water stop running downhill?
Answer: Once it hits the bottom

Riddle: When does a tennis player rise in the morning?
Answer: Ten-ish

Riddle: You enter a room filled with kings, queens, and twins. But you don't see any adult in it. How do you explain this?
Answer: The room is filled with beds.

Riddle: I am a chiropractor's favorite way to swim laps. What am I?
Answer: A back stroke

Riddle: When rain comes down, I go up. What am I?
Answer: An umbrella

Riddle: I have no body. I only have a tail and a head. What am I?
Answer: A coin

Riddle: What are black, gray, brown, purple, green, yellow, red, and blue?
Answer: A box of crayons

Riddle: What did Mr. Skeleton order for dinner?
Answer: Spare ribs

Riddle: After going to the bank, Dracula returned home very pale. How do you explain this?
Answer: Dracula went to a blood bank to donate some blood.

Riddle: What 3 keys can't open doors?
Answer: Turkey, donkey, and monkey

Riddle: Remove more from me and I become even bigger. What am I?
Answer: A hole

Riddle: You see me two times in a week, once in a year, but not even once in a day. What am I?
Answer: The letter "E"

Riddle: When does August come before February?
Answer: In the dictionary

Riddle: What do Halloween, Dracula, and Vampires have in common that a zombie doesn't have?
Answer: The letter A

Riddle: When a vampire goes for you in the middle of a blizzard. What do you get?
Answer: Frostbite

Chapter 8: Guess What

Riddle: You remove the outside. You then cook the inside. You eat the outside and discard the inside. What is it?
Answer: Corn on the cob. You remove the husk. You cook the corn. You eat the kernels. And then you discard the cob.

Riddle: You find one of us set in glass. Another, you can find in bed. You may find another in tin. The 4th you will surely see in box: and the last one, hides in the middle of a rug. What are we?
Answer: The vowels

Riddle: What word is always spelled incorrectly in the dictionary?
Answer: Incorrectly

Riddle: What do fish, birds, dogs, cats, and a scorpion have in common?
Answer: The letter S

Riddle: When I am new, I am black. When you use me, I turn red. When I am all used up, I am gray. What am I?
Answer: Charcoal

Riddle: You can hear me and catch me. However, you can't see me. What am I?
Answer: A Remark

Riddle: Stella is my sister but I am not her sister. Who am I?
Answer: I am Stella's brother.

Riddle: I don't get any wetter even when it rains really hard on me. What am I?

Answer: Water

Riddle: I smell like black paint. I pour out like blue paint. And I look like a yellow truck. What am I?
Answer: Yellow paint. Paint pours out and smells like all others. If it is the color of a yellow truck, then it must be yellow.

Riddle: I can point in all directions yet I can't go any place on my own. What am I?
Answer: Your finger

Riddle: I am as big as an elephant but I weigh nothing at all. What am I?
Answer: Its shadow

Riddle: Remove my skin. I will not cry. But you certainly will! What am I?
Answer: An onion!

Riddle: People have a great time telling, cracking, making, or playing me. What am I?
Answer: A joke

Riddle: I am very frail. Call out my name ever so softly and I get broken. What am I?
Answer: Silence

Riddle: You can never get rid of me. People who leave me behind discover that they still have me. What am I?
Answer: Fingerprints

Riddle: I have a head, a foot, and 4 legs. What am I?
Answer: A bed

Riddle: I am a time piece. But you don't need to wind me up. What am I?
Answer: A rooster

Riddle: I am the best thing that you can ever put in a pie. What am I?
Answer: Your teeth

Riddle: I start out tall at the beginning. As I continue with my job, I get shorter. What am I?
Answer: A candle

Riddle: At sunrise, I start out with 4 legs. I am left with just 2 legs at noon. The sunset, however, finds me with 3 legs. What am I?
Answer: A baby crawls on all fours. An adult walks. An old man needs a cane to support him.

Chapter 9: It Does Make Sense

Riddle: How far can a squirrel run into the forest?
Answer: The squirrel can run only up to the middle of the forest – and then it would run out of the forest.

Riddle: Say racecar backwards.
Answer: Racecar backwards.

Riddle: Two teams were playing baseball. One team won without any man touching base. How do you explain this?
Answer: The teams who were playing were all-girls teams.

Riddle: Every dictionary has me spelled wrong. What am I?
Answer: The word "wrong"

Riddle: Johnson is our town's butcher. He is six feet and seven inches in height. He wears size 10 shoes. What does Johnson weigh?
Answer: He weighs the meat he sells in his shop.

Riddle: What tree can fit into your hand?
Answer: A palm

Riddle: A girl pushes her car along the street and reaches a hotel. She then yells, "I'm bankrupt!" Why?
Answer: She is playing Monopoly.
Riddle: He has married a lot of women. However, he has taken no wife for his own. Who is he?
Answer: A priest

Riddle: Can a woman who lives in Canada be buried in the United States?
Answer: Why would you bury a woman who is still alive?

Riddle: Is it okay for a man in Texas to get married to his widow's sister?
Answer: If he has a widow, the man must be dead! How can he get married?

Riddle: Why do Japanese men eat less rice than Chinese men?
Answer: Because there are less Japanese men than Chinese men.

Riddle: I was 21 the day before yesterday. Next year, I will be celebrating my 24th birthday. How can this be?
Answer: Today is January 1. I was born on the 31st of December, which was yesterday. The day before my birthday (December 30), I was 21. Yesterday, I turned 22. On December 31 of this year, I will be 23. On December 31 of next year, I will be 24.

Riddle: (To be asked orally) What is white and black and red all over?
Answer: Newspaper is white and black and read all over.

Riddle: How many alphabets can you find in alphabet?
Answer: 8 (a-l-p-h-a-b-e-t)

Riddle: Why is it impossible to take a picture of a kid with his puppy?
Answer: Because you can't use a puppy to take pictures with. You need a camera.
Riddle: If you want a heavy metal box to weigh lighter, what should you put in it?
Answer: Holes
Riddle: What is the one thing that everybody does at the same time?
Answer: Grow old
Riddle: How should you drop an egg onto a floor made of marble without cracking it?

Answer: It is impossible to crack a floor made of marble with an egg regardless of how you drop the egg onto it.

Riddle: A building has five floors. One man lives on the ground floor but he doesn't use the elevator. Three men live on the 2nd floor, 5 men on the 3rd floor, two couples on the 4th floor, and a family of 5 on the 5th floor. What floor do you think calls the elevator the most number of times?
Answer: The ground floor, of course!

Riddle: I am lighter than a feather. However, no one in the entire world – not even the strongest man, can hold me for more than a single minute. What am I?
Answer: His breath

Riddle: I can go 30 days without sleeping. How is this possible?
Answer: I only sleep at night.

Riddle: If I run a race and overtake the person who is in second place, what place am I in?
Answer: Second place

Riddle: Why did the little girl bury her flashlight?
Answer: Because the batteries were all dead.

Riddle: Before going to bed, what is it that you take off last?
Answer: You take your feet off the floor.

Riddle: What happens to a black stone if you throw it into the Red Sea?
Answer: It becomes wet.

Riddle: If I do not have all my fingers on one hand, what do you call me?

Answer: Normal. Every normal person has fingers on both hands – not just on one!

Riddle: Which one of the football players wears the largest helmet?
Answer: The player with the largest head, of course!

Riddle: Why isn't there any nose that is 12 inches long?
Answer: Because it would no longer be a nose but a foot.

Riddle: Ann gets in the shower. When she comes out, she is as dry as can be. How do you explain this?
Answer: She didn't turn on the faucet.

Riddle: Johnson shaves many times a day. However, his beard is as full as ever. How do you explain this?
Answer: Johnson is a barber.

Riddle: Sally is a hair stylist. When asked which she would rather cut, one red hair or a couple of brunettes, Sally immediately said she preferred the brunettes. How do you explain this?
Answer: Sally earns more from giving two haircuts.

Riddle: What is going to happen if you swallow your spoon when you are having coffee?
Answer: You will not be able to stir your coffee.

Riddle: A little kid falls off a 30-meter ladder unhurt. How do you explain this?
Answer: The boy fell off the lowest rung of the ladder.

Riddle: How many pairs of animals did Moses bring with him on the ark?

Answer: Moses didn't take any animal with him. It was Noah who did.

Riddle: The more it dries, the wetter it becomes. What is it?
Answer: A towel

Riddle: You see a boat full of people across the bridge. And somehow, there wasn't a single person on board. How do you explain this?
Answer: Everyone on that boat was married.

Riddle: When you are looking for something, why do you always find it in the last place that you look at?
Answer: Because you stop looking immediately after you find it

Riddle (to be read out loud): One night, a prince and a princess went into a palace. No one except them was in the palace. No one left the palace. The morning after, three persons came out of the palace. Who were these three people?
Answer: The prince, the princess, and the knight (night)!

Riddle: A woman who lives in New York can't be buried in Chicago. Why is this so?
Answer: Because the woman still lives

Riddle: Tuesday, Claire and Maureen had lunch in a fancy restaurant. Claire and Maureen did not spend a single dime for what they ate. Who took care of the bill?
Answer: Tuesday, their friend

Riddle: Aside from the United States of America, what other country has the 4th of July?
Answer: All countries have the 4th of July – and the 5th, and the 6th, and the 7th.

Riddle: Two boys had the same mother. They were born in the same month and year and the same day and time. However, they weren't twins. How do you explain this?
Answer: They were part of a group of triplets.

Riddle: How did the soccer fans guess even before the game started that the score was 0-0?
Answer: Every game starts at 0-0.

Riddle: What is the first thing you should do if you come upon an alligator while you are swimming in the ocean?
Answer: You will not find an alligator in the ocean. Alligators are fresh-water animals.

Riddle: Four children and four cats stayed under a small umbrella. Why didn't any of them get wet?
Answer: It wasn't raining.

Conclusion

Thanks again for choosing this book!
I hope you enjoyed those riddles!
If you enjoyed this book, please take the time to leave me a review on Amazon. I appreciate your honest feedback, and it really helps me to continue producing high quality books.